Staying
ON
THE *Path*

Dr. Wayne W. Dyer

Hay House, Inc.
Carson, CA

HAY
HOUSE

098

Copyright © 1995 by Wayne W. Dyer

Published and distributed in the United States by:

Hay House, Inc.
1154 E. Dominguez St.
P.O. Box 6204
Carson, California 90749-6204

Edited by: Jill Kramer
Book design by: Highpoint Graphics, Inc., Claremont, CA

Library of Congress Cataloging-in-Publication Data

Dyer, Wayne W.
    Staying on the path/Wayne W. Dyer.
        p.   cm.
    ISBN 1-56170-126-2 (pbk.)
    1. Self-actualization (Psychology)—Quotations,
maxims, etc. I. Title.
BF637.S4D893   1995
170'.44—dc20   94-38239
                                               CIP

ISBN 1-56170-126-2

99 98 97 96 95   5 4 3 2 1
First Printing, February 1995

Printed in the United States of America

For my mother, Hazel Irene Dyer,
who used her magnificent vision and
intention to clear so many obstacles from
her own path — I love you.

Preface

I have created this book for those of you who are already on the path—as well as those of you who are just trying to get there. My observations may strike a chord in your life at present, or you might find that they come in handy a little way down the line. Whatever the case, just by picking up this book, you are already making headway on your own particular course.

May your journey be a safe and loving one.

— *Dr. Wayne W. Dyer*

*A*ll of us are on our own paths,
doing exactly what we know how to do
at the moment, given the conditions
of our lives.

*T*he measure of your life will not
be in what you accumulate, but
in what you give away.

*T*he secret of abundance is to stop focusing on what you do not have, and shift your consciousness to an appreciation for all that you are and all that you do have.

*P*ractice being in the world, but not of the world—learn to ignore how things outside of you are going, and know that higher awareness is truly a disappearing act.

*S*end out love and harmony,
put your mind and body in a peaceful
place, and then allow the universe to work
in the perfect way that
it knows how.

I don't have to be directed by anything outside of myself. God is within me, and the infinite and divine power that gives me sustenance as a human being is always there.

*Y*ou can never get enough of what you don't want.

You can't go around being what
everyone expects you to be, living
your life through other people's
rules and be happy and have
inner peace.

The only antidote to anger is to
eliminate the internal sentences, "If only you
were more like me" and "If only the world
were not the way it is."

*E*verything in your life is a miracle
to be cherished. A grain of sand, a bee on a
flower, a sailboat, a cup of coffee, a wet diaper,
a caterpillar, are all miracles....When you
learn to view life and everything in it
as a miracle, you soon see that
complaining is a waste of
the miracle that
you are.

*J*ust because a person is young or small
does not make him or her incomplete....
The truth is that we are complete at
all moments in our life.

*W*hen you become immobilized
by what anybody else thinks of you,
what you are saying is that your opinion
of me is more important than my
own opinion of myself.

When Wayne's daughter Tracy came
home in the second grade and said,
"Billy doesn't like me. Billy doesn't like me,"
Wayne responded, "Do you like you?"
Tracy said, "Yes." Then Wayne replied,
"Well, that's all you've got."
You see, even at 7 years of age, a person
shouldn't get the idea that anyone
else's reactions to you should in
any way get you down.

*D*id you ever notice how difficult
it is to argue with someone who is
not obsessed with being right?

*Y*our suffering comes from needing
things to be different. When you stop that,
your suffering stops. You can want things,
but it is the needing it that
must go.

*L*ife is an attitude. It's what you
choose to believe, always.

*Y*ou can come
to a beautiful temple
every Sunday, and you can practice all
kinds of Bible sayings, and you can label
yourself with the most fantastic tags that you
can come up with, but you won't find your
heart in a temple if you don't have
a temple in your heart.

*W*hy not think about some
things you've never done before and
do them just because you've never done
them and for no other reason?

A sense of purpose
is not something that you find;
it's something that you are. Truth is not
something that you look for; it's something
that you live.

*N*othing out there is bad unless
you believe that it is.

*I*f you choose not to respect your sense
of justice, you choose not to respect
yourself, and you will soon end up
wondering how much your
life is really worth.

*Y*our body is the garage
where you park
your soul.

*L*ife is never boring, but
some people choose to be bored....
Boredom is a choice.

*I*f you want to be confident,
but don't normally act that way, today,
just this once, act in the physical world the
way you believe a confident
person would.

*A*nything that keeps you from growing
is never worth defending.

*Y*our reputation
is in the hands of others.
That's what a reputation is.
You can't control that. The only thing
you can control is
your character.

*I*t's never too late to have
a happy childhood.

*T*here are two ways to look at
virtually anything. One is the violent way,
and one is the peaceful way.
It's the yin and yang of the universe.

*Y*our opinions are trivial,
but your commitments to them
make all the difference in the world.

*M*y belief
about compassion is summed up
by the old saying,
"Give a man a fish and he eats for a day.
Teach a man to fish and he eats
for a lifetime."

*W*hen you live on a round planet,
there's no choosing sides.

*T*he total being called human being
cannot function harmoniously
when the components
are in conflict.

*I*f enough of us shied away from conflict
and confrontation, just imagine how
much war we could eliminate.

You have a very powerful mind
that can make anything happen
as long as you keep
yourself centered.

You were a winner from the moment
you were born....There were several
hundred billion sperm in one glob chasing
this one egg. They were all in a race. The prize
was this egg, and they were all swimming as fast
as they could. There were billions of them,
and you won. You won the first race
you were ever in.

A non-doer is very often
a critic—that is, someone who sits back
and watches doers, and then waxes
philosophically about how
the doers are doing.
It's easy to be
a critic, but being a doer
requires effort, risk, and change.

*C*reativity means believing
you have greatness.

*T*he highest form of ignorance
is to reject something
you know nothing about.

*D*eath is merely a form of transformation.
Imagine what our planet would be like
without it. It's like taking off a
worn-out garment.

*A*s long as you stay
where you are and tell yourself
you have to do it because you've always
done it, the only payoff you get is
to defend your misery.

*O*nce you become detached from things,
they don't own you any longer.

*R*e-examine the sentence,
"Just do your best."
I would substitute it with,
"Just do."

*T*he elevator to success is out of order today.
You're going to have to take the stairway,
one step at a time.

There is no way to enlightenment.
Enlightenment is the way.
It's a principle of living rather
than seeking.

Every moment that you
spend upset, in despair, in anguish,
angry, or hurt because of the behavior
of anybody else in your life is a
moment in which you've
given up control
of your life.

*T*hroughout life, the two most
futile emotions are guilt for
what has been done and worry
about what might be done.

"*I*t's the space between the bars
that holds the tiger," as they say in Zen,
and it's the silence between the notes
that makes the music.

*E*verything that your form needs to house
this soul that you are wears out and changes and
dies, but the divine formless you
never dies.

*Y*our own expectations are the key
to the whole business of mental health.
If you expect to be happy, healthy, and
fulfilled in life, then that is where you'll place
your attention, and that is what
you will manifest.

*F*ailure is an editorial judgment
imposed by others.

*T*rue inner serenity will always elude
those who sit in judgment, since
they use up their life energy
in anger at what is.

*P*eople who have
behaved toward you in any way
that you find disagreeable truly
do not know what they have done to you
because they are living out of
their separateness.

*H*ow old would you be
if you didn't know
how old you were?

*F*ear itself does not exist in the world.
There are only fearful thoughts and
avoidance behaviors.

*T*here is no scarcity
of opportunity to make a living
at what you love. There's only a scarcity
of resolve to make it happen.

*B*e consistently aware
of the need to serve God
and to serve others in any
and all of your actions.
That is the way of the
miracle worker.

*E*very human being
who does any damage or inflicts
any pain on anybody else is a far
greater victim than those he victimizes
and must answer for all of those
things to a law of
the universe.

*E*verything we fight only weakens us
and hinders our ability to see the
opportunity in the obstacle.

*W*hat distinguishes what's alive from
what is dead is growth, be it in plants
or in you.

*G*uilt takes place in the present moment,
as does everything. It is a way
of using up the present moment
to be consumed with something that
has already happened, over which
you have no control.

*H*abits are changed by practicing
new behavior, and this is true for
mental habits as well.

*M*ost people are searching
for happiness. They're looking for it.
They're trying to find it in someone
or something outside of themselves.
That's a fundamental mistake.
Happiness is something that you are,
and it comes from the way that you think.

*T*he first step to healing
anything in your life
is to understand that whatever
disease process is going on
within you is something you carry around.
You own it all.
It's all yours.

*T*he people who get the most respect
in this world are those who are the
straightest, even though they often
take the most abuse.

*B*eing *against* anything
weakens you, while being *for* something
empowers you.

*Y*ou're the creator of your thought,
which means that in some metaphysical
way, you're the creator
of your life.

*I*t isn't the world
that makes you unhappy,
or the way people are in the world.
It's how you process the people and
events of our world.

*T*he antecedent to every action
is a thought.

*I*nstead of judging others as people
who ought to be behaving in certain ways,
see them as reflecting a part of you, and
ask yourself what it is you are ready
to learn from them.

*C*reate an inner harmony
where your loving soul guides your
physical behavior, rather than having
your soul always come in
second place.

*L*ive the Ten Commandments.

*T*he more you have a
harmonious, loving, accepting
approach, the more you will see the rest
of the pieces all fitting nicely together.

*O*ne of the most responsible things
you can do as an adult is to become
more of a child.

*H*onor this incarnation
and be fully alive.

A special kind of freedom
is available to you if you are
willing to take the risks involved
in getting it: the freedom to wander where
you will about life's terrain, to make all
your own choices.

Live...Be you...Enjoy...Love.

To change yourself,
look at what you fear
and what you hate.
Start there.

*Y*our circumstances
do not determine what your
life will be; they reveal what
kinds of images you have
chosen up until now.

*T*here are limits to material growth,
but there are no limits to
inner enlightenment.

*W*ithin you is the kingdom of serenity
that can create all of the prosperity that you
could ever want.

*W*hen you know
that you are in charge of your intentions,
then you will come to know
that you are in charge
of your entire world.

*J*ealousy is really a demand
that someone love you
in a certain way, and you saying,
"It isn't fair" when they don't.
It comes from a lack of self-confidence.

*I*f you refuse to change your job
(if you don't like it), the only sensible thing
you can do is practice
loving it every day.

*T*he only difference between
a flower and a weed is
a judgment.

*S*end out anger and impatience,
and that's what you'll get.
Send out love, and you'll get back love.

*Y*ou can set yourself up to be sick
or you can choose to be well.

The more you extend
kindness to yourself, the more
it will become
your automatic
response to others.

Observe yourself
and others in this nutty world,
and then decide whether to carry around
anger or to develop a sense of humor
that will give you and others
one of the most priceless gifts
of all—laughter.

$\mathcal{N}$o one, regardless of how much
he or she wishes it, can put understanding into
another human being. Understanding can only
come from doing.

$\mathcal{L}$ife presents itself to you
and asks nothing of you.
You can take life and swim deliriously
through it, or you can fight it.
But when you elect to spend your time
fighting it, you can't use
the same time
to enjoy it.

I can assure you that once
you no longer need the lessons in
your life that unpleasant events
offer you, you will no longer
have these events.

*T*hose who seem to cause you
the most anguish are those who remind
you of what you believe is either
lacking or wanting
in yourself.

*T*he more you stop to observe
and learn from animals, the healthier
a philosophy of life you are
likely to have.

*Y*our joy is divine
and so is your suffering.
There's so much to be learned
from both.

When you argue for your limitations,
all you get are your
limitations.

A lot of people have
bumper stickers that say,
"This is the first day of the rest of your life."
I prefer to think, "This is the last day
of my life, and I am going to
live it as if I don't
have any more."

*Y*ou're always alone,
but you're only lonely if you don't like
the person you're alone with.

*T*he "un" in *unconditional*
means not judging.

*W*e can never become awakened or
enlightened until we can move beyond form.
Every philosopher who ever lived
has taught that.

*Y*our love is located within you.
It is yours to nurture and savor. It is yours to
give in any way you choose. This is true for
others as well. If someone you love fails
to return the love the way you would
like it returned, that is the other
person's choice. It doesn't at all
detract from your love.

*P*eople generally stop
having hurt feelings when
they realize that those feelings
can no longer be used to
manipulate you.

*T*he measure of your life
won't be in what you accumulate;
it will be in what you gave.

γou must come in contact
with the empty space that lies within,
not the form that
encapsulates it.

When you think positive,
happy, loving thoughts, there's a different
chemistry that goes into your body
than when you think depressing,
negative, anguished thoughts.
The way you decide to think
has a dramatic effect on your chemistry
and on your physiology.

*Y*our miracles are an inside job.
Go there to create the magic
that you seek in your life.

*Y*our right to swing your fist stops
with my right to have my nose shaped
the way I want it.

*T*here's not one cell in your body today
that was there seven years ago.
Yet you can remember being there
seven years ago.
How do you account for that?

A flabby lifestyle is inexcusable.
All of your reasons for being out of shape
are nothing but excuses you make
to yourself.

*L*ooking into the mirror and
disliking the self that you take with you
everywhere you go is one of the most
self-defeating things
you can do.

*N*o-limit people
are so in charge that they can trust
their instincts, be childlike, be creative,
do anything that makes sense to them and
make their lives into what they
really believe they want
for themselves.

*S*t. Mark said,
"With God, all things are possible."
Now what does that leave out?

*T*he past is over for all of us.
The future is promised to none of us.
All we get is this one.
That's all we get.

*E*very obstacle that comes along
on this planet is either an opportunity
to grow and transcend our form and
think differently or to use it as
an excuse to believe
we are stuck.

*Y*ou are in a partnership with
all other human beings, not a contest
to be judged better than some and
worse than others.

*E*veryone deserves our love, and until
we start thinking that way, we're always going
to have us versus them thinking.

*E*ach problem
is an opportunity in disguise.

*I*t's not what is available or unavailable
that determines your level of success
and happiness; it is what you
convince yourself is true.

*I*f things are not working, ask yourself,
"In what way am I creating this?
In what way can I change?
What is the lesson?"

*H*elping somebody else achieve
a sense of purpose is a part of the mission
of what it means to be a parent.

*E*verything in life is a paradox.
The more you want approval, the more you
become a person that other people don't
want to approve of; the less you care
about whether you get approval, the
more you get.

*T*here's a big difference between
not liking someone's behavior and
not liking someone.

*T*ry to learn from the past,
rather than repeating it and making
references to it all the time.

*Y*ou can never please everyone.
In fact, if you please 50 percent of the people,
you are doing quite well.

*E*ach experience in your life was
absolutely necessary in order to
have gotten you to the
next place, and the next,
up until this very moment.

*W*hen the universe is presented with a problem, does it say, "I don't know how to deal with
this"? No. The universe is perfect.

*T*he only boundaries we have are in form.
There are no obstacles in thought.

*L*ove is forgiving
...and love is for giving.

*R*emember what Victor Hugo told us,
"Nothing is more powerful than an idea
whose time has come."

*A*ll of the "stuff" in your life
has arrived to serve you, rather than
to make you a servant
of the stuff.

*P*rejudice means to "pre-judge."
When you prejudge, you are making
a decision about something before you have
enough data on which to
base a decision.

*I*f you are a person who lives one way,
but who says you are going to live
another way in the future, those
proclamations are empty.

*T*here is no way to prosperity;
prosperity is the way.

*I*f you get pushed around,
you've been sending
push-me-around signals.

*W*hen you truly know
that your life has a grand and heroic mission,
you will realign yourself
as a spiritual being.

A purpose is not something
that you're going to find.
It's something that will find you.
And it will find you only when you're ready
and not before.

*Y*ou leave old habits behind
by starting out with the thought,
"I release the need for this in my life."

*T*hose who behave in ways that you
dislike are sending out their disharmony
toward you because that is what they have to
give away. Hating them is akin
to hating moss for growing
on the tree.

*T*he only limitations you have to
magical relationships are those you
have imposed upon yourself.

*I*n any relationship in which two people
become one, the end result
is two half people.

*Y*ou can reshape your thinking
so that you never have to think
in negatives again.
You and only you choose
your thoughts.

Risk is only our evaluation of it.

You have to risk some feelings
of insecurity if you are ever going to
learn to walk a tightrope, water-ski,
become a writer, start a new business,
try out a new recipe, or do
anything that requires learning.

*S*ome people believe that they live a life
of lack because they are unlucky, instead
of recognizing that their belief systems
are rooted in scarcity thinking.

*T*hey used to say to scientists,
"Do you believe in God?"
And the scientist would respond,
"No, I'm a scientist." Today, in the '90s,
if you ask a scientist, "Do you believe in God?,"
the scientist will say,
"Of course. I'm a scientist!"

*O*nly insecure people
need security. Secure people know
that there's no such thing. Security
comes from within, when you know
you can handle anything.

*B*e patient and loving with
every fearful thought.

*W*hen you are at peace with yourself
and you love yourself, it is virtually impossible
for you to do things to yourself
that are destructive.

*Y*ou cannot always be number one, or
always win a contest, or always get the merit
badge, or always make the honor roll, but
you can always think of yourself as an
important, worthwhile person.

*S*elf-esteem comes from the self, not from
acquisitions and approval.

*O*ur beliefs about ourselves
are the single most telling factors
in determining our success and
happiness in life.

*E*very single condition in your life
can be improved if you learn to be
more effective at visualizing what you
want and having the intention
to manifest it.

*I*ndividuals who use self-labels are stating,
"I am a finished product in this area, and
I am never going to be any different."
If you are a finished product, all tied up
and put away, you have
stopped growing.

*M*ake a personal decision to be in love
with the most beautiful, exciting, worthy
person ever—*you!*

*W*ith everything
that has happened to you,
you can either feel sorry for yourself,
or treat what has happened as a gift.
Everything is either an opportunity to grow
or an obstacle to keep you from growing.
You get to choose.

*W*henever other people are upset,
always remember that they own the upset,
and that you can refuse to join them.

*Y*ou must become the producer,
director, and actor in the
unfolding story of your life.

No one can depress you.
No one can make you anxious. No one
can hurt your feelings. No one can make
you anything other than what
you allow inside.

Don't equate your self-worth with
how well you do things in life.
You aren't what you do. If you are what you do,
then when you don't, you aren't.

Shy people make shy pictures over and over
in their minds, and until they see themselves
as unafraid, they will always act on the
pictures they create.

You do not have to be a person
who is at the mercy of anyone who chooses
to annoy you.

*W*hat makes you human
is not this form, but the invisible intelligence
that suffuses it—mind, spirit, God,
whatever you want to call it.

*I*magine the word CANCEL being a
huge rubber stamp in your mind. Stamp
CANCEL on any self-defeating image you
place in your head. If you think "poor me"
thoughts, you will CANCEL that
thought for the moment and begin
to think in some kind of a
self-enhancing way.

*S*uffering comes from wants.

*C*hasing success is like trying to squeeze
a handful of water. The tighter you squeeze,
the less water you get. With success, when you
chase it, your life becomes the chase, and
you never arrive at a place called *successful*.
You become a victim of wanting more.

*S*urrender to a new consciousness, a thought
that whispers, "I can do this thing in this
moment. I will receive all the help that
I need as long as I stay with this intention
and go within for assistance."

*W*e become what we think about
all day long. The question is,
"What do you think about?"

*O*ur days are the precious currency
of our lives.

*A*dvance confidently in the direction
of your own dreams to live the life that
you have imagined.
That's when you have success.

*M*editation gives you an opportunity
to come to know your invisible self.
It will shatter the illusion of your separateness.

*E*ach of us has a well of infinite depth
within us, which contains more potential
for creativity than we can
ever imagine.

*T*here is a rhythm to the universe.
When we are able to get quiet enough,
we experience how we are a part of that
perfect rhythm.

*I*f you find yourself being treated in
a way you resent or which turns you into
a victim, ask yourself this question: "What
have I done to teach this person
that this behavior is something
I'm willing to tolerate?"

*W*hen you get enough inner peace
and feel really positive about yourself, it's
almost impossible for you to be controlled
and manipulated by anybody else.

The use of mental imagery is one of the strongest and most effective strategies for making something happen for you.

You mustn't attempt to will anything. You need only be willing.

*H*ow do you get world peace? You get world peace through inner peace. If you've got a world full of people who have inner peace, then you have a peaceful world.

*E*verything I ever worried about turned out exactly as it was going to despite my worry moments to the contrary.

*A*ll that you need in order to have
total happiness, fulfillment, and love in
your life you already have right now,
whoever you are, wherever you are.

*Y*our body is perfect. It knows how
to do all the things that bodies are
capable of doing. It knows how to walk,
sweat, sleep, be hungry, cry....It is also a very
good learner. You can teach it to swim,
drive a car, write a letter, play a guitar,
cut a diamond, or climb
a mountain.

*T*he children whom you admire so much
for their ability to enjoy life are not
foreign creatures to you.
You have one of those children
inside you.

*D*oing what you love is the cornerstone
of having abundance in your life.

*E*verything that is happening
is supposed to be happening.

One of the really good exercises to do
to release attachments is to go through
your garage and your closets
and take all the things that the children
won't use anymore and give them away.
Have your children participate in this.

You can make your life
into a grand, ever-evolving work of art.
The key is your thoughts, the wondrous,
invisible part of you that is
your spiritual soul.

*A*nalyzing is really a violent intellectual act.
When you analyze something, you have to
break it apart and find every
little part of it.

*B*uddha said, "You will not be
punished *for* your anger. You will be
punished *by* your anger."

YOU control your emotions, so you
do not have to explode with anger
whenever someone else decides
to behave in angry ways.

Needing approval is tantamount to
saying, "Your view of me is more
important than my own opinion
of myself."

*A*rguing is really saying, "If you were really more like me, then I could like you better."

*L*oving people live in a loving world. Hostile people live in a hostile world. Same world. How come?

You can't be authentic
unless you're following
your bliss.

The path to the big picture is different
for everyone, but the understanding has to
be that the big picture is there, and its
availability is there.

*T*here are some people who live
70 years, and there are some people who
live one year 70 times, repeating what
they're doing over and over in the
name of the gold watch
or whatever.

*S*ince your mind is your own
private territory, you can give any new
idea a private audition for
a few days.

*I*f you're looking for love, it will always
elude you. If you're looking for happiness,
it will always elude you. When you become
these things, it is all you will have to
give away.

*B*elieve it and you'll see it.
Know it and you'll be it!

*S*top blaming your spouse for your
unhappiness, your parents for your lack
of motivation, the economy for your social
status, the bakery for your excess weight, your
childhood for your phobias, and anything
else to which you assign blame points.
You are the sum total of the choices
you have made in your life.

*T*he way you change your behavior
is to look at the source of strength
that you are.

*B*ehavior is a much better
barometer of what you are
than words.

A child is a wonder
to behold.

*F*eelings are not emotions that
happen to you. Feelings are reactions you
choose to have, and they show up in your
body as physical reactions to
your thoughts.

*I*f you don't have confidence in yourself,
get off your rear end and do anything
that will make you feel better
about yourself.

*I*f you practice maintaining your
composure, and remember that someone
else's behavior belongs to that person
and cannot upset you unless you allow
it to do so, then you will not become
an unwilling target.

*T*he opposite of courage
is not so much fear as
it is conformity.

I cannot always control what goes on
outside, but I can always control
what goes on inside.

*T*houghts are ways in which we can
make virtually anything happen.

*G*et your nose out of everybody else's garden.
Get your own in order, and stop focusing on
everybody else's. Grow what you want to
grow in your garden.

*Y*our form will simply pass along,
but you can't kill thought, so you can't
kill who you really are.

*T*he more you let go of people and
things, the fewer obstacles you will have
on your life's journey.

*T*he most effective weapon you have in ban-
ishing neurotic behavior from your life is your
own determination.

*I*f you believe that this book
will liberate you, then you are already
a victim of your own illusions before
you even start reading.
You and only you must decide to take
these suggestions and turn them into
constructive, self-fulfilling behaviors.

*S*chools must become concerned
and caring places full of teachers
who understand that teaching people
to love themselves, to feel positive
about their natural curiosity and
in control of their own lives
ought to be given at least
as much attention
as geometry and grammar.

Your emotions
shouldn't be immobilizing.
They shouldn't be defended.
They shouldn't keep you from being
all that you can be.

These are
the good old days.

*E*nlightened people
move away from conflict
and confrontation.

*I*f you believe that feeling bad or worrying
long enough will change a past or future event,
then you are residing on another planet
with a different reality system.

*H*ow harmony gets inside you
is through your own thinking.

*W*hatever it is that constitutes your very life,
it doesn't weigh anything. When life leaves
the package you showed up in,
the package weighs the same.
So your life is something other
than the package.

*W*hen you are told
that you have some kind of physical affliction,
you can either prepare to suffer
or prepare to heal.

*I*f you slip,
it doesn't mean you're less valuable.
It simply means you have something
to learn from slipping.

*F*ear of failure becomes fear of success
for those who never try
anything new.

*T*o not forgive
is to fail to understand
how the universe works and
how you fit into it.

The freest people in the world
are those who have
inner peace.

Give love and unconditional acceptance
to those you encounter,
and notice what happens.

An invisible intelligence
suffuses all form in the universe
and allows flowers to grow and planets to align
and the whole thing to exist.

The more you understand yourself
as a human being, the more you realize
that you can either flow with life or fight.
And every time you fight something,
you get weaker.

*E*nlightened people have perfect love in them
just like everyone else does;
the only difference is that they have
nothing else in them.

*G*uilt is an irresponsible choice.
As long as you feel guilty
about whatever you've done,
then you don't have to do anything
to correct it.

*H*ealthy thinking is a habit,
just like neurotic thinking
is a habit.

*H*appiness and success
are inner processes that we bring
to life's undertakings, rather than
something we get from
"out there."

*T*he body is a great healer.
That magnificent, perfect creation
is capable of healing itself in
many, many instances.

*I*f you expect to be upset,
then you will seldom
disappoint yourself.

*H*ighly functioning people say,
"Where I am is fine,
but I can grow."

*T*ry viewing everyone
who comes into your life
as a teacher.

*A*nything that bothers you
is only a problem within.
Only you can experience it,
and only you can correct it.

*I*n Zen they say,
"Before enlightenment, chop wood, carry water.
After enlightenment, chop wood, carry water."
You've got to chop and carry.
That's just part of the human condition.

*I*nstead of judging others
as people who should be behaving
in certain ways, see them as reflecting
a part of you, and ask yourself what it is
you are ready to learn from them.

*Q*uality rather than appearance...
ethics rather than rules...
knowledge rather than achievement...
integrity rather than domination...
serenity rather than acquisitions.

*I*t is intelligent to have a plan,
but neurotic to fall in love with it.

*P*erhaps the single most
outstanding characteristic of healthy people
is their unhostile sense of humor.

*I*f you want to find a deeper meaning
in your life, you can't find it in the opinions
or the beliefs that have been handed to you.
You have to go to that place
within yourself.

*D*evelop an inner candle flame
that won't flicker even when the worst
goes before you.

*I*ntention is the energy of your soul
coming into contact with
your physical reality.

*O*ther people
are going to be exactly
the way they are, independent
of your opinion of them.

*L*oving relationships work
because there is no work.

*W*hen you no longer need to learn
how to deal with disharmony in your life,
you will stop creating it,
and you will create love and harmony
virtually everywhere you turn.

*I*nstead of saying,
"Why is this happening to me?
Isn't this awful. Poor me,"
begin to say,
"What do I have to learn from this?"

*T*he only limits you have
are the limits you believe.

You are not your form.
You are something much more magnificent
and divine and grand.

Any time you get hate,
send out love.
Then love will come back,
and you will be free.

*T*hat we breathe,
that we showed up on this planet,
that we communicate,
is a miracle.

*N*etworking can never fail.
It's so powerful because you just keep creating
more power sources.
It's like geometric progression.

*T*he difference between
being a neurotic and a no-limit person
isn't whether someone has problems.
Everyone has problems. It's attitude.
Do you look for solutions or more problems?

*I*f you can conceive it in your mind,
then it can be brought into
the physical world.

The purpose of life is to know God.

If you work at living your life a moment—
instead of a decade—at a time,
then you can cope with
your problems.

The beggars in the streets of New Delhi,
the boat people in Malaysia,
the royalty in Buckingham Palace,
the factory worker in Detroit, and you
(whoever you are) are all equal cells
in the body called humanity.

Every problem you have
you experience in your mind.
The solution to the problem is in the same place.

*W*e are all at once teachers and learners
in every encounter
of our lives.

*I*f children are raised in peace,
they will not know how
to be warlike.

*W*hat's over is over.
You did what you knew how to do.
It wasn't right or wrong or good or bad.
It just was. But all you've got is today.
You can't have it back.

*S*tarvation is part
of what the universe is about,
but so is my desire to change it.

*N*o one can get behind your eyeballs
and experience life
the way you do.

*T*he only difference between *ALONE*
and *ALL ONE* is one *L*...
and that stands for *love*.

*I*n matters of taste,
you alone are, and must be,
the sole judge of what pleases you.

*E*verything you "have to have"
owns you.

As you awaken, you go beyond
the need to accumulate and perform and achieve.
When you go beyond it,
you begin to develop an increased susceptibility
to the love extended by others as well as
the uncontrollable urge to extend it.
Love becomes what you are.

It takes not one drop of sweat
to put off doing something.

When God speaks through your hands
and smiles upon the earth through you
because you are an unconditional giver,
a purposeful being, asking nothing of anyone,
prosperity will be your reward.

The moments between events
are just as livable as the
events themselves.

The more space you allow and encourage
within a relationship,
the more the relationship
will flourish.

When you have the choice
between being right and being kind,
just choose kind.

The War on Drugs isn't going
to work...because it's a war.

If you don't believe
that you control your thoughts,
make a list of who does.
Send them to me.
I will treat them all,
and you will get better.

*T*he entire gamut of human experience
is yours to enjoy once you decide
to venture into territory where
you don't have guarantees.

*S*ecurity is ugly.
Security is self-defeating. Security is boring.
Security is dull. What do you want security for?

*B*eing self-actualized
means being able to welcome
the unknown.

*T*aking care of yourself
is a natural outgrowth of self-love.
Have a quiet love affair with yourself.

*I*f you're in a relationship with someone
who is treating you in a rude and obnoxious way,
you have to say, "What do I think of myself?
Why have I allowed this behavior to persist?"
And "Am I going to allow it to continue?"

*O*nce you begin working
on your problem areas with small,
daily success-oriented goals for yourself,
the problems disappear.

*I*f you don't love yourself,
nobody else will.
Not only that, you won't be good
at loving anyone else.
Loving starts with the self.

*Y*ou don't need to let anyone in your life
unless they come in with
love and harmony.

One of the highest places
you can get to is to be independent
of the good opinions of other people.

Circumstances do not make a man,
they reveal him.

*I*f you accept full responsibility
for conducting the symphony of
all your thoughts and feelings,
you will have to listen to the whole orchestra.
You cannot just march to the drumbeat
of external orders.
You also have to listen to the strings of
your conscience, to the voice of the child
within you, and to all other voices of
internal origin that you are
privileged to conduct.

*S*elf-worth cannot be verified by others.
You are worthy because you say it is so.
If you depend on others for your value,
it is "other-worth."

*I*n western civilization,
we're accustomed to believing
that what we produce and what we get
for ourselves is a measure of who we are,
when, in fact, that's a spiritual dead end.

*H*appiness, fulfillment,
and purpose in life are all inner concepts.
If you don't have inner peace and serenity,
then you have nothing.

*O*nly a ghost wallows around in his past,
explaining himself with descriptors
based on a life already lived.
You are what you choose today,
not what you've chosen before.

A successful person
is not a person who makes a lot of money.
A successful person brings success to everything
that he or she does, and money
is one of the payoffs.

*Y*our ability to be a winner
100 percent of the time
is based upon giving up the notion
that losing at anything is equivalent
to being a loser.

*I*f you are suffering in your life right now,
I can guarantee that it is tied up
with some kind of attachment
to how things should be going.

*Y*ou are doomed to make choices.
This is life's greatest paradox.

Once you know
that what you think about expands,
you start getting real careful about
what you think about.

When you are ready,
whatever you need to be transformed
will be there.

*T*he more you work at just being yourself,
the more likely you'll feel purposeful
and significant in your life.

*W*hen you're just like everyone else
in the world, you have to ask yourself,
"What do I have to offer?"

The universal principles
will never show up in your life
until you know they're there.
When you believe them,
you'll see them everywhere.

You don't get abused because
there are a lot of abusers out there.
You get abused because you send out signals
that say, "Abuse me. I'll take that."

What you have to learn to do
is to fall in love with what you do
and then sell that love.

You can spend the rest of your life,
beginning right now,
worrying about the future;
and no amount of your worry
will change a thing.

*Y*ou are whole. You are complete.
You are total in every moment
that you are alive.

*A*bundance is about looking at life
and knowing that we have everything we need
for complete happiness,
and then being able to celebrate
each and every moment of life.

*W*hen you *know* rather than *doubt*,
you will discover the necessary ability
to carry out your purpose.

*T*o enter the world of real magic,
you must enter the dimension
of spirituality.

*A*ll that you fight weakens you.
All that you are *for*
empowers you.

*T*here is no anger in the world.
There are only angry thoughts.

*T*he next time you get nervous
about others' opinions, look them mentally
in the eye and say, "What you think of me
is none of my business."

*D*id you ever notice
that some people never have enough,
and other people always have enough?

The winning attitude
is one that allows you to
think of yourself as a winner all the time
while still giving yourself
room to grow.

As you become awakened,
you're not ego-defined anymore.
You're not defined by *what I get and how I get it.*
You're more defined by *I can be more internally*
at peace and *How can I help other people do that?*

*B*e a student.
Stay open and willing to learn
from everyone and anyone.
Being a student means you have
room for new input.

*P*eople need to be right.
If you can get that out of your life,
you'll save yourself lots
of suffering.

*W*hat do you think is the difference
between a child who can swim
and one who can't?
Do you think that the moment a child
knows how to swim he or she has new
physical capabilities?
No, it's just a new belief, and the child
is acting on that belief.

*A*nybody can change completely
and become anything he or she wants to become
in moments.

*E*ven in a prison,
your corner of freedom
is how you choose to think.
No one can take that away ever!

*Y*ou don't have to continue
to behave the way you have behaved,
just because you always have.

*Y*ou can't kill thought.
It's eternal.

*I*f you think of yourself
as an important person,
you will not allow yourself to be overweight
or suffer from any eating disorder.

*Y*ou do it. You do it.
You don't say, "I can't do it."
You DO it!

*S*omehow we've got this notion
that life is a dress rehearsal.
It isn't. This is it!

You can have no inner peace
as long as the controls of your life
are located outside yourself.

Babe Ruth struck out
more than anybody in the history of baseball
the year he hit 60 home runs.
Do you want to hit home runs?
You'd better be willing to strike out a lot.

*I*f you believe it will work out,
   you'll see opportunities.
   If you believe it won't,
   you'll see obstacles.

*S*end all your enemies love.
It's easy to love some people.
The true test is to love someone
   who's hard to love.

*F*orgiveness is the most powerful thing
you can do to get on the spiritual path.
If you can't do it, you can forget about
getting to higher levels of awareness
and creating real magic in your life.

*T*here is no such thing
as a well-adjusted slave.

*W*henever you are tempted
to give less, try giving
a little extra instead.

*G*uilt means that you use up
your present moments
being immobilized as a result
of past behavior.

*H*ealthy habits are learned
in the same way as unhealthy ones—
through practice.

A woman asked me one time,
"What are the blocks to my happiness?"
I said, "The belief that you have blocks."

*L*isten to your body,
and it will tell you what
you need to know.

*I*f you take two sentences
out of your life:
"I'm tired," and "I don't feel well,"
you will have cured about
50 percent of your tiredness
and your illness.

*O*nce people know
you are intimidated by their anger,
they will use it to victimize you
whenever it will work.

*Y*ou become
what you think about all day long,
and those days become
your lifetime.

You get treated in life
the way you teach people
to treat you.

If you build a house
that has as its foundation
only one support system
and that particular support collapses,
your entire house will topple.

*L*ove the seemingly opposites
in your world; treasure their way
of being as a gift to you.

*G*ive up the want; know that you
do not need one more thing
to make yourself complete,
and then watch all those external things
become less and less significant
in your heart.

*S*hift your focus from
What's in it for me? to *How may I serve?*

*T*he key to being effective
and awake in our lives
is to be students rather than teachers

*I*f you are pessimistic
about anything or have any hatred or dislike
in you, that is the place to go to work.
That is the evidence that you aren't living
with a temple in your heart.

*T*o live your life the way you choose,
you have to be a bit rebellious.
You have to be willing
to stand up for yourself.

*B*eing relaxed, at peace with yourself,
confident, emotionally neutral, loose,
and free-floating—these are the keys
to successful performance
in almost everything.

*I*nner development is just as important
as outer physical development.

A gold watch
at the end of a 50-year career
with one company is no compensation
if you disliked yourself and your job
for all those years.

*T*he only difference
between someone who's beautiful and
unattractive is a judgment.
There's nobody in the world who is unattractive.
No one on this planet. Unattractive is just
what people decide to believe.

*E*xamine the labels you apply to yourself.
Every single label is a boundary or
a limit of one kind or another.

*D*etachment is one of life's great lessons
for those on the path
of enlightenment.

Your joy is divine and so is your suffering.
There's so much to be learned
from both.

Your lifetime in form
is to be honored and celebrated.
Go beyond your enslavement
and live fully in the now,
the only time you have.

*I*f you don't take time
for your exercise and health now,
then you will have to take time later.

*I*f 90 percent of doctors
don't believe in the mind-body connection,
how do they wiggle their toes?

*N*eurotics are looking for problems.
They want things to get worse.
They want to be right.

*Y*ou are always a valuable,
worthwhile human being,
not because anybody else says so,
not because you're successful,
not because you make a lot of money,
but because you decide to know it.

The NOW is a magical place
where you are uniquely capable
of being so involved that there is no room
for any unhappy or debilitating thoughts.

The way to oneness seems to be through
the path of inner harmony.
The way to inner harmony is through thought.

*I*f you think that the solution is outside
of yourself, but the problem is inside of yourself,
then you're living an illusion.
The fact is that every problem is in your mind,
and so is every solution.

*A*s Carl Jung reminded us, at the same
moment that you are a protagonist
in your own life,
you are a spear carrier or an extra
in a much larger drama.

Children need to know that the words
"It's impossible" are not a part of your vocabulary
and that you are a supporter
of their dreams.

You'll hear psychiatrists talk about
living in the past. No one can live in the past.
You can only live in the now, using up now
by reminiscing about the past,
or feeling bad about the past.

*E*verything that happens to us
has a blessing built into it.

*M*ore is less.
For me, having more means having to insure it,
protect it, polish it, worry about it,
try to double it, brag about it,
price it, maybe sell it for a profit,
and on and on.

If you're always in a hurry,
always trying to get ahead of the other guy,
or someone else's performance
is what motivates you,
then that person is in control of you.

You overcome old habits
by leaving them behind.

*T*he only way you'll ever quit smoking
is to not put cigarettes in your mouth
one day at a time.

*W*hen you come to another
with love in your heart, asking nothing,
only offering that love,
you create miraculous relationships.

*T*he state of your life
is nothing more than a reflection
of your state of mind.

*A*s long as you are willing
to stay as you are or to stay only with the familiar
and not take risks and try new things out,
then it is, by definition,
impossible to grow.

The next time you are contemplating
a decision in which you are debating
whether or not to take charge of yourself,
to make your own choices,
ask yourself an important question:
"How long am I going to be dead?"

Rather than fretting
about your past or future relationship
with your parents, try to be as pleasing
and interested in them as you can—today!

*G*iving love to others is directly related
to how much love you have
for yourself.

*W*hatever is going on inside of you
is up to you. You own it all.
It's yours.

*S*ex is a participatory dance of creation.

*A*ll of the things
going on in your physical life
are just going on.
There is a part of you
that is changeless...eternal.

*N*inety-nine percent of us is nonform,
and we are almost obsessed, it seems,
with the one percent that is in form.
We spend most of our energy in the one percent,
looking at each other's packages.

*W*hen the holiday season comes along,
put a sign on your bathroom mirror
that says very emphatically:
NO ONE IS GOING TO RUIN
THIS SEASON FOR ME...
ESPECIALLY YOURS TRULY!

There is no *path* to success;
success is an inner attitude
that we bring to our endeavors.

Make cooperation and service the rule
in all your business dealings.

You have the power to think
whatever you choose to allow into your head.
If something just pops into your head,
you still have the power to make it go away.
Therefore, you still control your mental world.

Great things have no fear of time.

The person looking back at you in the mirror
is the one you have to answer to
every day.

You go out into the world,
and you are who you choose to be,
and you know that some of the people will like it
and others won't.

*T*he universe works on many principles
that are beyond our control.
They work independent of our opinion about
them and work even if we do not
understand them.

*B*eing a victim is a habit.

*W*orry is a means of using up
the present moment in being consumed
about something in the future, over which
you have no control.

*I*nner perfection is there
for each one of us to recapture.

*I*nstead of getting mad at the world
for the way that it is, let's accept it
and do what we can
to improve it.

I am going to become more
present moment-oriented,
enjoying each activity for itself
instead of thinking about
what is ahead for me.

*T*he state of the world
is nothing more than a reflection
of our minds.
And the state of our individual lives
is also a reflection of our state of mind.

*I*f others hurt you, let the injury go.
This is your test. If you let it go,
you will find serenity.

*I*f you are love, and you live love,
and you send it out, there will be so much love
in your life that you won't know
what to do with it.

*N*eurotics say,
"If only you were more like me,
then I wouldn't have to be upset
at you right now. If only you were
something different than what you are,
then I could be happier in my life.
If only oil prices hadn't gone up...
If only unemployment weren't the way it is...
If only...If only..."

You have the power to become anything
that you want to. Set your expectations
for yourself, and know that you will become
whatever you think about.

You are unique in all the world.

We're all on the same path.
We're just on different places along the path.

About the Author

Dr. Wayne W. Dyer is one of the most widely read, internationally renowned authors in the field of self-development today. He has written numerous bestselling books (*Everyday Wisdom, Your Erroneous Zones, Real Magic, Your Sacred Self*), is featured on a number of audios and videos, and has appeared on over 5,200 television and radio programs, including *The Today Show, The Tonight Show, Phil Donahue,* and *Oprah.*

We hope you enjoyed this
Hay House book.
If you would like to receive a free catalog
featuring additional
Hay House books and products,
or if you would like information about the
Hay Foundation, please write to:

Hay House, Inc.
1154 E. Dominguez St.
P.O. Box 6204
Carson, CA 90749-6204

or call:

(800) 654–5126